THE NUTCRACKER

A **CURTAIN-RAISER** BOOK

The Nutcracker

E.T.A. HOFFMANN

Illustrations by

DAGMAR BERKOVÁ

J.M. DENT & SONS LTD

LONDON

This edition first published in Great Britain by
J.M. Dent & Sons, Ltd. and in the United States of America by
Franklin Watts, Inc., 1968. All rights reserved.
No part of this publication may be reproduced or transmitted in any form or by
any means without permission in writing from the publisher.
Illustrations © 1968 Artia, Prague
Text by E. Petiška (based on the original story by

E.T.A. Hoffmann) © 1968 Artia, Prague
Reprinted 1970
English version based on translation by Olga Kuthanová
Designed and produced by Artia
for
J.M. DENT & SONS LTD.
Aldine House, Bedford Street,
London WC2
and
FRANKLIN WATTS, Inc.
575 Lexington Avenue, New York, N. Y., 10022

Printed in Czechoslovakia by Svoboda, Prague
S 2716

SBN: 460 05901 7

THE STORY AND THE BALLET

THE NUTCRACKER or *Casse-Noisette* (the music is always known by the French title) is one of the three famous ballets written by the great Russian composer Peter Ilyich Tchaikovsky, the other two being SWAN LAKE and THE SLEEPING PRINCESS.

The story of the ballet was based on the tale by Alexandre Dumas, himself inspired by one of the fantastic stories of E.T.A. Hoffmann, the German writer; it was choreographed by Lev Ivanov. Ivanov's libretto was not a great success and as a result THE NUTCRACKER is staged today in various versions.

If you go to see the ballet, do not expect to find the whole story given as it is told in this book. The ballet is really a *divertissement* on the theme; it opens with the children's party, then follows a dream in which the toys defeat the mice and Clara is taken to the Land of Sweets. There is nothing in the ballet about Princess Pirlipat nor about the hard nut Krakatuk.

But although the ballet has less story, the same fairy-tale charm is there. Good is pitted against evil, and right prevails in the end. It is an entertainment children love — and no wonder, for the principal characters are boys and girls like themselves, playing with dolls and toy soldiers.

THE NUTCRACKER had its world première in Russia at the Mariinsky Theatre, St. Petersburg in 1892 with choreography by Lev Ivanov. It was performed for the first time in England at the Sadler's Wells Theatre in London on January 30th, 1934, revived and staged by Nicholas Sergeyev. Alicia Markova and Harold Turner danced the principal roles.

THE NUTCRACKER was first performed in the U.S.A. in October 1940 by the Ballets Russes of Monte Carlo with Markova and Eglevsky dancing the principal roles.

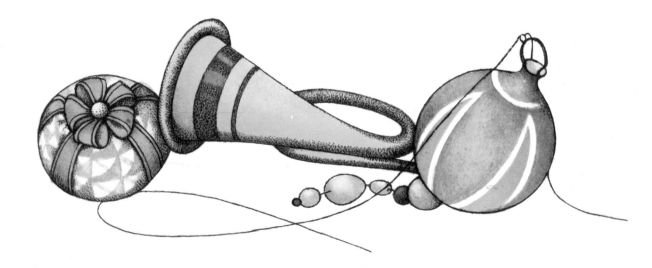

THE NUTCRACKER

Christmas Eve. Delicious hot smells of baking waft from the kitchen and mingle with the sharp scent of lemons and oranges and the cool fragrance of the fir tree which stands patiently with its foot in a pot and its arms outspread, being decorated. The room is a litter of sticky tape and scissors, teacups and stepladders, paper chains, tinsel and holly.

All day the family has been busy but now there is a pause. The preparations are nearly finished. For the children it is bedtime. They are tired but excited by the general air of expectancy and the thought of secrets they cannot bear to wait for any longer. Yet somehow wait they must — until tomorrow when Christmas really begins.

No ordinary, short bedtime tale will do for the children on this Christmas Eve. It must be a very special tale of fairies and princes and magicians — part of the enchantment that seems to fill the air tonight and haunt them like faraway music. The story of Clara, Frederick and the Nutcracker is the very thing. It happened long ago in the time of our great-grandfathers, or maybe even before that, and it is a Christmas story.

Frederick and Clara lived in a large and beautiful home. Every year when Christmas came around a great many friends and relations were invited to spend the evening with them, and this was when the presents were given out.

Frederick and Clara and the other small guests had not been allowed into the big drawing-room yet. Their father was hanging bright glass ornaments and candles on the tree and their mother was tying up the last packages with gay ribbons and laying them under the branches. All that needed to be done now was to light the candles. The children were eager to come in but they had to wait behind the locked door until their parents were ready. Frederick tried to peep through the keyhole but the key was in the way and he couldn't see a thing.

The big clock on the wall said that now it was time. *Bong-bong, bong-bong* it chimed, and the owl sitting at the top flapped its wings at every stroke. It looked as if it were trying to fly away, but could not, for it was made of wood and was part of the clock. Indeed, this was a remarkable clock, the only one of its kind, made by the children's godfather, Uncle Drosselmeier.

Behind the door excitement mounted and the noise grew louder as more children joined Clara and Frederick — the children of their parents' guests, who were invited every year and spent Christmas with them.

At last! Mother unlocked the door and Frederick was

the first one in. He was a rushing boy and always wanted to be everywhere first. Clara and the others followed on his heels, the grownups standing by the door smiling at the excitement.

The tree, covered from top to bottom with flickering candles, glowed in magnificent splendour and under its spreading branches lay a huge pile of gifts. Oh what a lot of packages! Some tiny, some enormous — where should they begin? As soon as the children had all their gifts they tore off the wrapping paper and spread the presents all over the floor — building sets, dolls, tin soldiers, picture books; and every child received a box with a gay costume. Laughing and shouting, they put on their fancy dress and were suddenly transformed into Chinese children, Spanish bullfighters, shepherds, milkmaids, clowns and fairies. Then they all started dancing.

As if attracted by the laughter and noise a small wrinkled man in a black morning coat suddenly appeared in the doorway. As soon as Clara caught sight of him, she called out, "Uncle, uncle," and ran to him with arms outstretched. He caught her up and kissed her. This was her beloved Uncle Drosselmeier. He could hardly be called handsome — he was small and thin and wore a black patch over his right eye. But Clara liked his hair: it was nice and long and white as snow. Not that it was his own — he was wearing a wig. Nonetheless, even if he was small and wrinkled and had to wear a wig because he hadn't any hair, he was still the best uncle in the whole world. He never came to see them without bringing something, and as for Christmas time, he gave the most beautiful presents of all. The toys he gave, however, weren't bought in a shop; he made every single one of them himself and the children believed there was not a thing in the world he could not do. If they weren't afraid to use the word, they would have said he was a magician.

Uncle Drosselmeier entered the room just as the clock on the wall began to chime, and the owl welcomed him with flapping wings. Behind him came footmen bearing

10

two large boxes. One was for Clara, the other for Frederick.
Uncle Drosselmeier kept an eye on them to be sure the
footmen didn't get them mixed up. The first one was for
Clara. It was so big — what could it be? Maybe a whole
model castle with towers and turrets and dozens of
windows just like the one uncle gave her last Christmas. When you looked inside through the windows you
could see tiny lords and ladies dancing and strolling

beneath silver chandeliers to the tinkling tune of a music box. And standing by the castle gate was Uncle Drosselmeier himself — a tiny little man no bigger than your finger.

Clara jumped up and down and clapped her hands in excitement as the footmen removed the lid and took out a large head of cabbage. Was that all? Just a head of cabbage? But no, the next instant it split in two and out jumped a big doll.

And what was in the other box that the footmen had placed in front of Frederick? Only a huge meat-pie? Yes, but it, too, suddenly burst open and out leaped a soldier in a handsome red coat. Then Frederick's soldier bowed low to Clara's doll, and the two began to dance.

Everyone was amazed at how beautifully they danced. None of the guests had ever seen such toys before in their lives. Only Uncle Drosselmeier could invent such wonderful things.

But a sad fate lay in store for these lovely toys. In those days many grownups thought children were always certain to damage anything precious. The doll and soldier had barely finished their dance when the children's father said:

"Beautiful toys, really much too beautiful, Uncle Drosselmeier, much too beautiful for little boys and girls. They might tear something or break them. Best to put them away so that nothing can happen to them." He turned to the footmen, saying, "Take them away!" and the footmen obeyed him, for his word was law.

Clara and Frederick were not at all happy at having their new toys taken from them. What sense was there in getting gifts that had to stay on the shelf? There was nothing worse than toys they weren't allowed to play with.

Their uncle felt sorry for them.

"Look," he said, "I still have something else here. Something that won't break easily. A present for the two of you." And with these words he put his hand beneath his coat-tails and pulled out a wooden soldier in grenadier's uniform and riding boots. He looked rather funny because his head was much too big for his body and when his wooden coat-tails were lifted he opened his mouth wide, revealing two rows of gleaming white teeth.

"Who is that?" asked Clara in surprise.

"That, my dear Clara, is Nutcracker," replied her unele. "He's called that because that's what he does — he cracks nuts, and very nicely too." With these words Uncle Drosselmeier put a nut between Nutcracker's teeth, pressed down on his coat-tails and the nut split with a sharp crack.

Clara liked the little fellow in the grenadier's uniform even if he did have a too-large head. If she could have put him in the room with her dolls she would have done

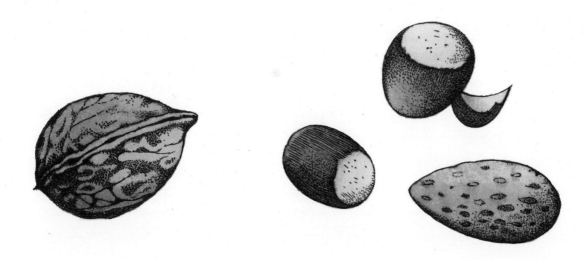

so right away. But he was not only hers, he belonged to Frederick too. She must let her brother have him for a while.

Frederick thought Nutcracker a great joke. "Some soldier!" he snorted. You might wonder what he knew about soldiers, but actually he knew quite a lot, for in the corner cupboard he had a whole company of tin soldiers with cannons drawn by horses and he was their commander. The cupboard had glass doors and at that moment all those soldiers were watching Frederick and Nutcracker.

"I wouldn't *think* of taking such a soldier into my company," he said, "but at least he'll be good for cracking nuts. Go on, crack them. Faster, faster!" he cried as he shoved nuts between Nutcracker's teeth one after the other as fast as he could. Finally he picked the largest one from the pile, put it in Nutcracker's mouth and pressed down on his coat-tails. *Cr-r-a-a-ck!* However, this time it was not the nut but Nutcracker's teeth that had given way.

"Oh, you horrid boy!" cried Clara, the tears welling up in her eyes. "You've broken him, and now his teeth are going to hurt."

Clara knew very well how painful a toothache could be. No wonder she felt so sorry for Nutcracker. As for Frederick — well, he just stood there and laughed at them both.

"He wouldn't have been any good as a soldier anyway," he said, for he judged everything from a commander's point of view. Clara, however, was not the com-

16

mander of an army and so she stroked poor Nutcracker's head, wishing she could help him. People go to bed when they are ill! Oh, why hadn't she thought of that before! Quickly she took her doll out of the little bed and lay Nutcracker down in it, tucking the blanket up under his chin so that he shouldn't catch cold. Then she took the white ribbon out of her hair and wrapped it around his head. Clara's mother always wrapped her head in this way when Clara had a toothache.

Suddenly she heard a sound of scurrying and she thought she saw a small dark shape dart across the floor.

"A mouse!" she cried in alarm.

Frederick was scornful. "Clara's afraid of mice," he said to Uncle Drosselmeier.

"There's no need to be frightened, Clara," her godfather told her kindly. "Mice won't hurt you unless their king is with them."

Clara guessed that her godfather had a story to tell about the mouse king. She would ask him to tell it one day when there were no guests to interrupt them.

She turned back to Nutcracker who lay stretched out in the bed, covered and bandaged, and it seemed to Clara as if he were crying.

"Don't," she consoled him, "don't cry. Shut your eyes and sleep. You'll feel much better in the morning. Your toothache will be gone by then, you'll see."

Nutcracker looked as if he understood and so Clara told him about when she had a toothache and how she went to the dentist, and about the presents she got for

18

Christmas. And then she told him a story her mother told her once — a nice, long story that made the time pass. And the minutes ticked by as she talked.

Somehow, time flies by faster at Christmas. All of a sudden the evening was over. The guests were saying goodnight and the lights on the tree were going out one by one.

"Clara! Frederick!" their father called. "It's late. Time to go to bed."

"What about Nutcracker?" asked Clara. "Can I take him to bed with me?"

"Leave him here with the toys," replied her father. "He doesn't belong in the bedroom. He'll still be here

in the morning. By the time you wake up he'll have had a good rest and then you can play with him."

Clara didn't want to leave Nutcracker — she had been having such a nice time talking to him. But there was nothing to be done. Father was standing in the doorway waiting and it was no good hoping that he would relent. Off she went to her bedroom. Father put the lights out and closed the door behind him.

Outside, the snow-covered houses huddled together in the velvety darkness of the night beneath a sky bright with the light of the crescent moon and myriads of twinkling stars, rivalling the glitter of the Christmas tree. A long shaft of moonlight fell on the floor as if the moon wanted to read what was written in the picture book Frederick had left lying on the rug.

All was quiet, the whole house was asleep. Only Clara lay awake, thinking about her Nutcracker, wondering how he was. She kept tossing and turning from one side to the other until finally she slipped out of bed and softly tiptoed to the door of her room. She opened it slowly, then shut it behind her, taking care not to make a sound, and crept downstairs.

The clock was just chiming midnight, the room was filled with silvery moonlight which penetrated to the farthest corner. Clara suddenly heard the sound of laughter and looked up. There on the clock, in place of the owl, sat Uncle Drosselmeier, his coat-tails waving

21

and flapping like the wings of a raven with each stroke of the clock.

"What are you laughing at, Uncle?" asked Clara.

But he didn't answer and suddenly she felt frightened, wondering whether she shouldn't run back to her warm, cosy bed.

Looking about, her gaze fell on the Christmas tree which to her surprise seemed to be growing bigger and bigger, the bells hanging from its branches tinkling merrily, the paper windmills turning round and round, and the glass birds opening their bills wide and singing. The tree had suddenly turned into a dense green thicket filled with the sound of bells, bird song and music.

"Oh how wonderful!" sighed Clara.

The china figures on the sideboard yawned and stretched their arms as if they were waking from a long sleep and saying: "It's time to get up and go to work". The china blacksmith brandished his hammer, the flower-girl arranged the flowers in her basket and the musketeer drew his sword. Even the gingerbread figures, which had been lying forgotten on the edge of the sideboard, jumped up, slipped down to the floor and started marching towards the tree, attracted by its chimes and music.

The toy cupboard was filled with bustling activity too. Behind the glass Frederick's tin soldiers were marching along the shelf just like real soldiers — left, right, left, right, left, right. The dolls, whose room was next to the soldiers' training field, were gazing out of the window not paying the slightest attention to Nutcracker who lay motionless in his bed.

"I wonder how he is, poor little chap," said Clara to herself. But she couldn't seem to find the strength to go and see. She stood rooted to the spot as if bewitched, looking around her without moving.

On the bottom shelf of the toy cupboard was where Teddybear slept. He had just got up and put his shoulder to the door. With a push the door opened and a sound of music drifted in; someone seemed to be playing the violin.

A startled cry escaped her lips when Clara noticed the open door. What if Nutcracker should fall out!

She was just about to go and shut the cupboard door when a strange sound made her pause. "That isn't the sound of Christmas bells," Clara said to herself, "and it isn't the soldiers' trumpets either."

From all sides she heard a weird rustling, scraping and squeaking, soft at first but getting louder and louder all the time. The queer squeaking sound coming through the walls and the floor soon drowned the music of the Christmas tree. From the cracks between the floorboards and where the floor meets the wall, gleamed the bright eyes of scores of mice. The boards cracked and the plaster gave way as their sharp little teeth gnawed holes through which they surged up into the room until it was full of squeaking mice. The gingerbread figures rushed towards the tree but the mice attacked them on the way and devoured them. Then the furry little creatures paused, twitched their noses, and looked around to see if there was anything else good to eat.

Clara couldn't take her eyes off the milling crowd of grey coats and long tails.

Now, as if in answer to a silent command, the mice lined up in rows like Frederick's tin soldiers and started marching in formation — one-two, one-two.

Clara could not help smiling at the sight but at that instant such a terrifying squeak sounded at her feet that it sent chills up and down her spine. The floorboards gave a sharp crack as huge sharp teeth bit into them from below. It must be an extremely big mouse that was trying to get into the room. It was. A mouse with seven heads pushed up through the pile of shavings around the hole in the floor. Clara quickly jumped up on the table to escape, for mice can't climb up on tables. They were running here and there all over the floor — but the minute the large mouse with seven heads appeared in their midst they stood to attention and gave a smart salute.

The big mouse gave itself a shake and as the dust settled Clara noticed that it was wearing a gold crown.

"This must be the Mouse King!" she exclaimed.

"Hurrah!" cried the army of mice and then they paraded in orderly ranks before their king and commander.

"I hope they won't hurt Nutcracker," said Clara to herself, her eyes seeking the shelf where he lay in his bed. Now began a great to-do in the toy cupboard. Out climbed bears, donkeys, elephants and bunny rabbits and lined up in nice neat rows. It was as if all the toys wanted to play soldiers, too. Then came the dragoons and artillery.

Gathered under the table on which Clara was perched was the army of mice making a horrible din with their squeaking. But what had become of Nutcracker, where was he? His bed was empty. The blanket had fallen out

and no-one had bothered to put it back. The dolls were scurrying back and forth, packing their belongings into boxes and suitcases. Were they really thinking of running away?

Oh *there* he was, there was Nutcracker! He had let himself down to the floor. The ribbon Clara had tied around his head was now a bright sash across his chest, and in his hand gleamed a small silver sword.

"Nutcracker!" Clara cried.

Nutcracker looked up and waved his sword as if telling her not to worry. Then he turned to the soldiers and she heard him say, "Those wicked mice must be driven out of Clara's house." After that she heard no

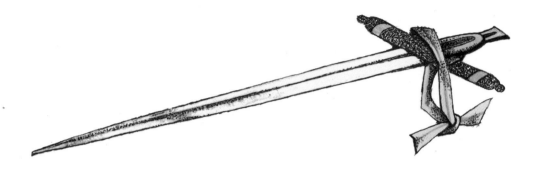

more because the squeaking under the table was getting louder and louder. The mice were evidently preparing to do battle.

Frederick's soldiers were ready too. The animals and puppets — the jester, knight, prince and night-watchman — all stood to attention in front of the cupboard. Hurrying to join them were the musketeer and the blacksmith from the sideboard. And just in time. The mouse army had begun to move, advancing towards the cupboard, its lines spread out across the whole room — from the sideboard to the tree.

Nutcracker's trumpeters sounded the call to arms while the tin soldiers pointed their cannons at the oncoming mice.

Boom! Boom! The cannons roared, the mice squeaked, the drummer beside the cupboard beat a sharp *rat-a-tat-tat*, the trumpeters blew their trumpets, the donkeys

30

brayed, the blacksmith brandished his hammer, hitting out at the mice right and left, and the soldiers fired their rifles.

The battle raged to the noise of banging, squeaking, shouting and the clash of weapons until Clara had to plug her ears, and now and then even shut her eyes. She was afraid to look at Nutcracker in the midst of the fray, giving orders and brandishing his sword. What if something should happen to him?

The fiercest warrior of them all was the Mouse King. Everything that came his way was crushed between his teeth; none of Nutcracker's men could do a thing about it. He pressed forward unhindered, rapping out orders in his high squeaky voice — until he stood face to face with Nutcracker. He crouched ready to pounce while

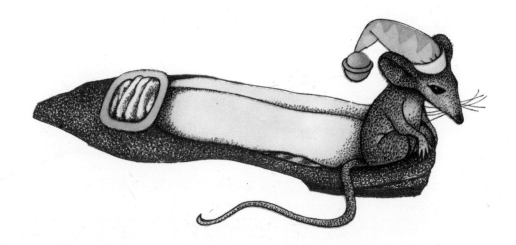

Nutcracker, lunging with his sword, tried in vain to stab him.

Clara, terrified, cried out:

"Nutcracker! Nutcracker!"

Quickly she pulled the slipper off her foot and hurled it at the Mouse King. Suddenly the noise died away and Clara fell to the floor in a faint.

All was quiet in the toy cupboard. A few scattered soldiers and the abandoned cannon on the rug were the only signs of the battle that had raged there shortly before. The dolls were seated in their room and the china blacksmith and musketeer were back in their places on the sideboard. But Nutcracker was nowhere to be seen. Where Nutcracker had stood now stood a handsome young prince. He leaned over Clara, holding a scented handkerchief to her nose to bring her out of her faint. Slowly she opened her eyes.

"Who are you? Where's Nutcracker?" she asked.

"*I* am Nutcracker," said the Prince. "I don't know how to thank you for saving me from the Mouse King. You are the one who broke the spell that bound me."

"The spell?" said Clara. "What spell? Tell me about it!"

"It's a long, long story," the Prince replied, "but come, come with me to my kingdom. I'll show you things no-one has ever seen before, and on the way I'll tell you."

Could anyone resist going with a handsome prince

to a fairy-tale kingdom where no human being had ever set foot? So Clara put her hand in his and as they approached the tree all she said was: "But please take a short road to your kingdom. You see, it's late already, and I must go to bed and get some sleep."

The Prince gripped Clara's hand as if he were afraid it might slip out of his grasp and together they climbed the branches of the Christmas tree. Or rather, they weren't climbing but floating amidst the glossy green of the fir needles, amidst the glittering ornaments and sugar plums wrapped in silver foil, deeper and deeper between the branches into a green and silver twilight. Snowflakes drifted softly down about their heads, each bright as a star and breathing a delicate scent.

"Oh, how beautiful!" cried Clara.

"This is a Christmas-tree forest," the Prince told her, pointing to the fir trees decked with fruit and silver chains — the bells in their topmost branches swaying in the soft breeze and filling the air with their music.

The snow fell softly and silently, blanketing the trees and making them look as if they were covered with white icing, and scurrying to and fro were dwarfs with bright-coloured caps carrying Christmas candles which, surprisingly, burned with a steady flame, lighting the way for Clara and the Prince.

Every now and then it seemed to Clara that she glimpsed a fairy-tale figure amongst the snowflakes — suddenly Puss-in-Boots would appear before her, over

there she saw fairies dancing in a ring, Snow White running to hide in the forest and Cinderella riding by in her coach.

"I keep seeing fairy tales wherever I look," she told the Prince.

"Why, of course, a Christmas-tree forest is full of fairy tales," he explained. "No doubt my story about Princess Pirlipat is somewhere amongst them, too. If you wish, I'll tell it to you. As a matter of fact it's the story I promised you — the one about myself."

"Oh do tell it, do!" Clara begged.

And so the Prince began:

Many years ago a daughter was born to the King and Queen of a kingdom beyond fairy-tale mountain. She was given the name Pirlipat and was the love-liest of all the children ever born in that realm. You can believe me when I say that, Clara, for I saw her with my own eyes . . . But that comes later.

All would have been well if the King hadn't had the unfortunate idea of inviting all the neighbouring knights, princes and kings to his annual feast. This was no ordinary feast, for the Queen herself cooked the soup in a golden kettle, and all the pots and pans, ladles, knives and forks were of silver, and the table on which the Queen prepared her special dish — seasoned sausages stuffed with bacon bits — was of silver and gold.

These sausages were the King's favourite dish.

And because she wanted to please him, the Queen took special pains, measuring out the ingredients with the greatest care and chopping and cutting whatever needed to be chopped or cut with her own two hands.

She was just cutting the bacon into tiny little pieces when she heard a squeaky voice from under the kitchen table saying:

"Give me a piece of bacon, just a wee piece."

"Of course I'll give you a piece," said the Queen, for she was a generous soul and this was a festive day when all the King's subjects should fare well, even the mice. (She had no idea that the mouse carrying off the piece of bacon was the Mouse Queen and that her sons were mouse princes.)

Hardly had they tasted the bacon when all the sons, nephews and nieces decided they wanted some more. They ran up her skirts and on to the table, eating up every bit in sight before you could say Jack Robinson. All that was left was one small piece and the poor Queen, though she tried her best, could not quite make it go round. She was left with one sausage without any bacon at all. That will have to be mine, she said to herself. I'll be sure to know which one to take.

The harassed Queen cooked the sausages, arranged them on a platter, then the chief royal steward carried them to the banquet hall. The noble company of kings, princes and knights took up their knives and forks, their mouths watering in anticipation. But the instant the King put the first morsel in

his mouth he turned deathly pale and cried out: "Bacon! There isn't any bacon in my sausage!"

The Queen had to come out with the truth and told him what had happened in the kitchen when she was cutting the bacon.

"How dare they!" roared the King in anger. "Mice! Mice daring to touch His Majesty's property! I'll show them! They won't get away with this!"

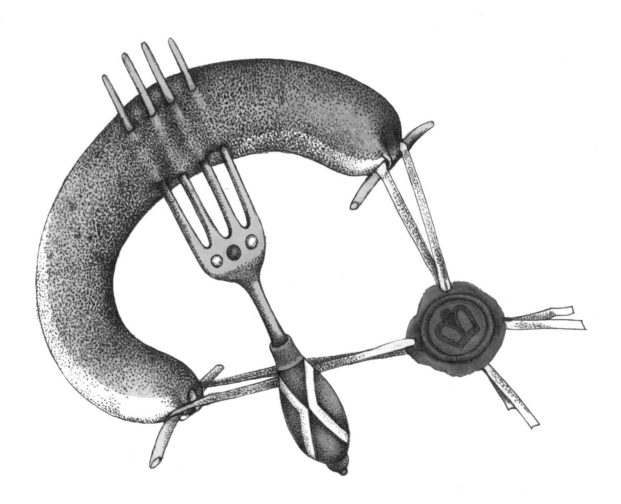

As is right and fitting in a ruler the King considered that anything that disturbed his comfort was a crime.

Luckily there lived at the castle the King's Court Inventor and Master Watchmaker, whose name was Drosselmeier — just like your uncle's. (Luckily for the King, that is, but not for the mice.) Drosselmeier the Watchmaker made several ingenious traps, and baited them with the bacon the mice liked so much and waited.

In vain did the Mouse Queen warn her princes, nephews and nieces of the danger. The smell of the bacon was too much for them. And so the Watchmaker caught all the mice in the castle, all, that is, except one — the Mouse Queen.

One day when Pirlipat's mother, the Queen, was again cutting bacon to make sausages for the King she heard a loud squeak from under the table, just as before.

"You killed all my sons, nephews and nieces," squeaked the Mouse Queen. "Take care, for I shall have my revenge! Take good care of your daughter Princess Pirlipat."

The good Queen was frightened out of her wits and so she hurried to the King and they summoned the King's wise men. The wise men together with the King, and the King together with the Queen decided that soldiers should stand guard outside Pirlipat's door day and night and that seven nursemaids should sit beside Pirlipat's cradle, each with a large cat in her lap. The King put great faith in the cats, for cats can smell mice from afar and would surely pounce on the Mouse Queen the minute she came close to the nursery.

Everything was well planned, nothing and no-one could get to the Princess past all those guards, and yet the thing everybody feared did come to pass. How it happened no-one knew, but one night all the cats fell asleep on the nursemaids' laps, and the nursemaids fell asleep and — strangest of all, for every one of them was an experienced soldier — even the guards at the door fell asleep.

On the stroke of midnight, when everyone was asleep and all was quiet in the castle and the cats were having the loveliest dreams, one of the nurse-maids suddenly woke up and saw a huge mouse standing beside the cradle in which Princess Pirlipat lay. She screamed but before she could gather her wits and before the other nursemaids had rubbed the sleep out of their eyes the mouse had vanished in a dark corner of the room. The King's wise men found the crack through which the Mouse Queen had entered but that was of no use to anyone, least of all to the poor little Princess, who from the instant the mouse touched her was completely transformed. Her body shrank and her head grew large and wooden, with a huge mouth — right there before everyone's horrified eyes. All that remained of the little Princess's former beauty was her pearly white teeth.

When the Queen saw what an ugly creature lay

there instead of her beautiful little daughter, she wished herself dead. The King wept and wrung his hands in despair.

"Send for the Court Watchmaker!" he shouted. "It's all his fault! If he had made really good mouse traps, he would have caught all of them — even the one that's hiding somewhere in this castle."

When his men brought Drosselmeier before the King he said to him: "You have three days to find a cure that will restore Princess Pirlipat to her former beauty. If you do not have an answer by that time, we'll cut off your head!"

"That's bad," said the Watchmaker to himself, "that's very bad. Mending clocks is one thing, but mending people is something I've never done in my life."

But the king's orders are the king's orders. And so he went into the nursery, sat down beside the cradle and gazed at Princess Pirlipat for a long time. So also did many famous doctors — all of whom finally shook their heads sadly and had nothing to say.

To make things worse, the poor Princess kept crying and screaming and nothing would calm her. The Watchmaker noticed what lovely teeth she had. "With those teeth she could crack nuts," he said to himself. And then out loud he said: "Bring the Princess some nuts."

The nursemaids brought a whole basketful of nuts and the minute she saw them Pirlipat stopped

crying, took one in her hand, cracked it between her teeth and ate the juicy kernel. And so she went on — cracking one nut after another until there weren't any left. When the last one was gone the crying and screaming began again. The nursemaids rushed to fill the empty basket, and Pirlipat cracked nuts from morning till night.

The Watchmaker sat and watched for a day and a night and yet another day, thinking and thinking and thinking. "Can it be that there's some secret hidden in those nuts?" he asked himself.

When there was only one more night left he got up and began looking in his books — heavy, old, learned books — and he pointed his telescope at the stars to see what they had to say about the Princess's fate. It was no easy task, for the Mouse Queen had made a really good, strong spell, taking pains to mix everything up so that it would last a long, long time. But the Watchmaker wouldn't give up until the books and stars had revealed their secret. When morning came, the guards took him before the King.

"Your Majesty," he said, "the Mouse Queen's spell will be broken if the Princess eats the sweet kernel of the rare and wonderful Krakatuk nut."

"Splendid, splendid!" cried the King, dancing with joy and smiling for the first time since the tragedy.

"The only thing is," continued the Watchmaker, "we have to find the nut first — which won't be easy — and then we have to crack it — and that's

44

not easy either. The Krakatuk has the hardest shell of all nuts in the world. We must look for a young man who will crack the nut between his teeth in front of the Princess. And the rules of this magic are that it must be a young man who has never yet shaved, and he must give the nut to the Princess with his eyes shut. Then he must take seven steps backwards, and only then open his eyes."

When the King heard what the Watchmaker had learned from the books and the stars he could hardly wait.

"Go," he said, "go and find the Krakatuk. And don't come back without it."

Oh Clara, you have no idea what a difficult task it is to find the Krakatuk. It is such a rare nut that no-one knows anything about it. It makes no difference where you start looking for it, in the east or in the west, it's never there!

The Court Watchmaker wandered over the whole wide world asking everyone he met, examining all the

trees that grew nuts and searching in the market places where nuts were sold, but no-one knew anything about the magic nut.

And so he went on and on until he finally came to China. One day as he was walking through a Chinese forest the poor, tired Watchmaker felt suddenly discouraged and seized with a great longing to see his homeland and he said to himself: "No matter where I seek I get the same answer. Who knows if there is or ever was such a nut as the Krakatuk? Anyhow, if there is one, maybe someone has already cracked it open and eaten the kernel."

And so the Watchmaker turned his back on the forests of China and set out on his return journey. He took good care to avoid all roads that led through the unhappy kingdom, for if someone were to recognize him and discover that he was coming back without the nut, that would be the end of him.

When, one dark night, he finally came to his home town the first person he visited was his cousin, who made puppets and knew not only everything there was to know about woodcarving and painting but everything that went on in the town, too. The Watchmaker told him what had happened to him in the King's service, all about the sad fate of Princess Pirlipat and about the Mouse Queen. When he had finished telling about his travels in search of the Krakatuk his cousin burst out laughing.

"What a lucky thing you came to me," he said to the Watchmaker, and with these words he took

46

down a box from the shelf, opened the lid and showed
him the nut that lay inside.

"Here is your nut," he said. "Here is Krakatuk."
And then he told of how the nut came to be in his
hands.

"Why, only last Christmas," he said, "two fellows
selling nuts got into an argument in front of my shop.
As they stood there shouting at each other, the nuts
from one of the sacks spilled out all over the road
just as a large wagon loaded with crates and barrels

was going by. The weight of the heavy wheels crushed the nuts as if they were made of paper and when the wagon had passed all that was left of them was a pulpy mass. But in the midst of that pulpy mass I suddenly spied a nut — the only nut that had remained whole. Just fancy — the heavy wheels had rolled over it and it hadn't cracked!

48

I thought it rather odd and I don't know why, but I bought that nut. I took it home and when I looked at it more closely guess what I found — the name Krakatuk clearly written on the shell in fancy letters."

And that's how the Watchmaker found in his own home town the nut he had been seeking throughout the whole wide world.

Now he had the nut, but he still had to find someone who would crack it.

I wouldn't want you to think I was boasting, Clara, but at least three hundred boys tried to crack Krakatuk in front of Princess Pirlipat, but all they did was to break their teeth. (The dentists in the city had their hands full.) When the Watchmaker saw them fail, one after another, he finally sent for the son of his cousin the woodcarver. And, as you may have guessed, that was *me*. Everything was arranged. I was a goodlooking boy, and I felt sure I would be able to break the horrible spell for the Princess because no-one in the whole street or in the whole town or in the whole country, for that matter, could match me for cracking nuts.

At the castle everyone had given up hope that someone who could crack Krakatuk would ever turn up when my uncle arrived with me.

"Your Majesty, this is my nephew," he said, introducing me to the King. "Let him try his luck. He's so wonderful at cracking nuts that everyone in our town calls him The Handsome Nutcracker."

The King clapped his hands and the footmen brought in Krakatuk on a plate. I put it between my teeth, clamped down hard — and the shell cracked! I took out the kernel, shut my eyes and handed it to the Princess. All that remained to be done was to take seven steps backward with my eyes shut. I was just about to take the last step when I heard the shrill squeak of a mouse behind me, and as I put my foot down I stepped on it, faltered and almost fell. At that instant my eyes flew open and I saw standing before me Princess Pirlipat with lovely pink and white skin and golden hair — as beautiful as she had been before the Mouse Queen had cast her spell.

But this time it was *I* who was suddenly changed. I had opened my eyes before finishing the seventh step backward and so the spell was switched to me. My body shrank, my head swelled and my mouth grew big and wide. I had been turned into a nutcracker — a real nutcracker for cracking nuts.

Naturally, I did not stay at court. My face would only have reminded the lovely Princess and the King and Queen of the days of their great unhappiness.

I might have remained a nutcracker for the rest of my life if I hadn't found my way to your Christmas tree — and to you, Clara.

After this new tragedy my uncle, the Court Watchmaker, sat down to study his ancient books and the stars in the heavens until he found what he was looking for — how to break the Mouse Queen's spell.

50

"My dear Nutcracker," he said, "the spell will be broken only if you slay the Mouse King who recently became the ruler when the Mouse Queen died. You must kill him in battle — and a young girl must help you do so. She mustn't mind your ugliness. She must help you because she loves you. If you find such a girl you will become your former self, and what is more, you will become the prince of a fairy-tale country."

And so it came about. It was *you*, Clara, who saved my life. If it hadn't been for you I would have remained a wooden nutcracker until my jaws finally broke and I was thrown out onto the dust heap."

Clara blushed at these words of praise and was filled with thankfulness when she thought of how he *might* have ended. But out loud she said: "Oh what a lovely smell! What is it that smells so nice?"

"That's the smell of Orange Brook," answered Prince Nutcracker.

Clara had been so fascinated by his story that she had forgotten to look about her. They had left Christmas-tree forest far behind and were walking together over a lush, emerald green meadow, their feet barely touching the ground. Alongside them burbled Orange Brook filling the air with its scent of fresh orange juice and with slices of orange bobbing amidst the ripples, looking just like small goldfish.

"Oh how lovely," cried Clara, "how perfectly lovely!"

She didn't mean just the smell of oranges but also the music, light, airy and sweet, which played softly as they drifted down the emerald meadow, each blade of grass sounding its delicate note as their feet touched it.

The Prince took her hand. "Give a push with your foot, Clara, a good push." And with that they both rose high above the meadow and floated through the warm blue air above the brook.

"We're flying! Oh, Prince Nutcracker, we're flying!" cried Clara in amazement.

"Yes. We're flying to make the journey shorter," he said. Then he pointed downward. "Look, that's Lemon

River down there below us. We still have to cross that before we reach our destination."

The yellow glare from the river made Clara blink. Soon the air was filled with the scent of lemons, which reminded Clara of her mother, for that was the smell that filled the whole house before the holidays when she was grating lemon rind for the Christmas cakes and pies.

"Shall we be there soon?" asked Clara. "I shouldn't like mother to be worried about me."

"Yes, in just a little while," the Prince replied. "We'll take a boat across Rose Lake right to the city gates. We could fly over the lake, but I'm afraid you might get dizzy. The smell of the waves in Rose Lake is even stronger than that of Orange Brook or Lemon River."

With that Clara and the Prince alighted on the shores of the lake which smelled like a rose garden. There just before them was a large shell, drawn by two golden dolphins. The shell was as big as a boat and was decked with precious gems whose bright flashing hues were reflected in the waves.

Out of the shell leaped six little boys, no bigger than the chocolate boys on the Christmas tree. They spread out a large carpet covered with golden coins — but before Clara could ask if the coins were filled with chocolate off they went, flying over the waves. The dolphins sped along so fast that the water on either side of the boat was churned into foam.

The little boys sang and danced until they set the shell rocking.

Clara laughed and laughed. "What fun, it's just like being in a swing." She was surprised that she wasn't afraid. Suddenly, as Clara gazed into the water, she glimpsed a lovely girl's face as if it were reflected in a hundred mirrors.

"Pirlipat, Pirlipat," she cried.

"No, that isn't Pirlipat," said the Prince, "that's *you*, Clara."

Once again Clara blushed a deep pink, but she was flattered and glad that she looked like a princess. The only thing she could not understand was how it could have happened. (However, as everyone knows, anything can happen in a fairy-tale land.)

Suddenly the city gates towered before them.

"Look, the guards are already waiting," said the Prince.

Clara didn't know where to look first. Spreading out before her was a city with sugar towers and turrets, streets

paved with candies, and gingerbread gates. In front of the gates in the shade of chocolate trees, whose branches were laden with jellies and sweetmeats, stood the silver soldiers of the municipal guard. As Clara and the Prince stepped out they gave a smart salute and the little boat boys played a fanfare on the small drums and trumpets they'd pulled out from somewhere. As if at a given signal all the sugar, gingerbread and candy windows in the town flew open and out of every one leaned a doll. Some were wearing paper gowns and others were dressed in brightest silver foil. All of them clapped their hands and cried out:

"Long live Prince Nutcracker! Hurrah! Hurrah!"

Clara and the Prince were greeted at the gates by a noble lord dressed in a handsomely embroidered coat. He led them to the beautiful sugar castle. The people waved and shouted as they passed and the streets were filled with music and dancing.

The noble lord walked in front making way for them between the dolls and snowmen.

"Oh-oh-oh!" breathed Clara when they came to the steps of the sugar castle.

It was a very big castle, much bigger than the one Uncle Drosselmeier had given her and Frederick last Christmas. His was a doll's castle, but this one was big enough for Clara to go into.

The castle glowed brightly. The roof and turrets sparkled as if covered with the stars of all the Christmas trees in the world. The noble lord struck the ground three times with his gold-tipped cane and the gates of

the castle opened. Out marched twelve pageboys, each bearing a large bouquet of flowers. They stood in two rows, casting blossoms on the path to make a soft, fragrant carpet for Clara and the Prince to walk on as they went into the castle.

"What a pity to trample such beautiful flowers," Clara said.

"You needn't feel so sad," said the Prince, "look behind you."

Clara turned and stood still in astonishment for the flowers they had walked over were standing upright again. And growing in their footsteps were roses, carnations, daisies and bluebells which swayed gently in the breeze, beckoning Clara to come and pick them.

After the pages danced four beautiful Princesses, who greeted Prince Nutcracker with tears and embraces and shouts of joy.

"Our brother, our dear, dear brother."

When the Prince finally managed to free himself, he took Clara by the hand and said to them, "My beloved sisters, this is Clara. It was she who saved my life when I fought the Mouse King."

Upon hearing this the Princesses rushed to embrace her, and showered her with thanks. Such a display of emotion made Clara feel shy and she was quite glad when they led her inside the castle where a feast had been laid out for them in the banquet hall.

Prince Nutcracker sat at the head of the table and told all about his many adventures, while the pages served Clara's favourite dishes. Nut rolls, nut bars and marzipan sweets on large crystal platters which glittered as if carved from ice. And there was everything to drink — orange juice, lemon juice and raspberry juice served in tall, crystal goblets — and many more delicious things. Then the Princesses cut her a slice from a huge cake decorated with a picture in sugar and chocolate icing of Nutcracker's battle with the Mouse King and topped with a large, big candy slipper just like the one that belonged to Clara. Then, of course, there was cocoa, chocolate or tea to drink with the cake.

At the height of the festivities Prince Nutcracker stood up and said: "Dear Clara, if you would like to come and live with us here in this castle, it would make me and my sisters very happy."

"I should love to stay," replied Clara, "but I must go home first — to get some sleep, and tell my mother all about everything. After that I'll come back."

And she will go back one day, she really will, she will return to the fairy-tale land where Prince Nutcracker rules with Princess Pirlipat (for he wooed and won her). If not tomorrow, then on Christmas Eve when father and mother are trimming the tree and the whole house is filled with the pungent fragrance of fir and holly and the delicious hot smell of baking cakes and pies.